When Animals Sleep

Story by Karen Cogan
Illustrations by Marianna Tcherepanova-Smith

At night, mouse hunts for seeds.

He sleeps when bluebird
wakes up to sing.

At night, bat hunts for mosquitoes.

He sleeps in his cave when
cow wakes up to eat grass.

At night, rabbit nibbles
in the garden
when the farmer is in bed.

She sleeps in her burrow when
horse wakes up to eat hay.

Some animals sleep at night.
Some animals sleep in the daytime.
When do you sleep?

After the Last Page...

Activities that can extend this book into other areas of the curriculum or into the home are endless. Here are just a few ideas. Have fun!

- Draw a picture of your favorite place to sleep.

- Read about nocturnal animals. Choose one to research. Share your findings with the class.

- Make a graph of nocturnal and diurnal animals that live near your house.

- Make a list of animals you would like to stay up and watch at night. Tell why.

Seedling Publications, Inc.

ISBN: 1-880612-98-4
72 Words